He Cares,
He Comforts

Jesus Is Victor

He Cares,
He Comforts

CORRIE TEN BOOM

FLEMING H. REVELL COMPANY
OLD TAPPAN, NEW JERSEY

Library of Congress Cataloging in Publication Data

Ten Boom, Corrie.
    He cares, He comforts.

    (Jesus is victor)
    1. Consolation. I. Title.
BV4905.2.T46   242'.4   77-8260
ISBN 0-8007-0891-1

Contents

Preface

Through my traveling over the world, and through my books and films, I have made many friends. When they are ill, I should love to be able to visit and comfort each of them. But I do pray for them, and the Lord gave me this idea—to write them a letter!

That was the beginning of this book. I prayed that the Lord would guide me and give me the thoughts, remembering what I had experienced with sick friends, and He gave me one after the other.

Often friends have the same problem, the same kind of suffering, and that's why I wrote down all I could remember. I'm sure that when a friend is sick, he or she will find in one of these stories an answer that the Lord has given me when I needed it.

It is the Lord who has helped me to remember. So I hope that my friends will read this book as a message that the Lord gave—to me, for them.

Dear Friend,

You are one of the many people who know me, perhaps even one of the many I have met on my recent journeys, an acquaintance who read one of my books, heard me talk, or saw me on film. And so there grew a real fellowship between you and me. I asked the Lord to give me an opportunity to meet you and He gave me this privilege of writing. He caused me to remember visits, experiences that I had with other sick people, and I'm sure that in these you will find an answer to the question *Why?* or to another problem that you have to face.

My friends had to endure suffering and now you are in the same kind of trouble. I prayed to the Lord to give me a word of comfort and an answer and I wrote them down. I think one of these stories that I tell may be an answer for you, from Corrie, but given to Corrie by the Lord Himself. Oh, it was wonderful that the Lord gave me the thoughts and the answers so quickly! So

in some way it is a greeting, a message from the
Lord Himself, who loves you and has your life in
His hands, who knows of every suffering, every
problem, as no human being does.

If you do not know Him, this book will be a
challenge, an invitation from the Lord, who said:

> Come unto me, all that . . . are heavy laden,
> and I will give you rest.
>
> Matthew 11:28

And if you know Him already, it will be a message from that Friend you and I have in Jesus.

Perhaps you are too ill, too weak to talk much
with Him, but then you may lay your weak hand
in the strong hand of Him who said:

> . . . him that cometh to me I will in no wise
> cast out.
>
> John 6:37

How He loves you!

"Jesus Heard You . . . ."

Jesus heard when you prayed last night.
He talked with God about you.
Jesus was there when you fought your fight,
He is going to bring you through.

Jesus knew when you shed those tears,
you did not weep alone.
The burdens you thought too heavy to bear,
He made them His very own.

Jesus Himself was touched by that trial,
you could not understand.
Jesus stood by as you almost fell
and lovingly clasped your hand.

Jesus cared when you bore that pain,
indeed, He bore it too.
He felt each pain, each ache in your heart,
because of His love for you.

Jesus, your Saviour, will always be with you,
no need to be anxious or fret.
Wonderful love, He will be there all the time,
He has never forsaken you yet.

1

That Wee Little Baby

Yesterday I met a lady who is expecting a baby. I always like to pray with such a mother and to pray for the baby she has under her heart.

"Lord Jesus, You love that baby already. You know it and You can already fill that tiny little heart with Your love. Lord, will You give the baby and the mother strength and health for the time of pregnancy? And also for the birth? Bless the doctors and the nurses and give them wisdom and love." I was happy that I could pray with that mother, for I know that the Lord hears our prayers.

Some time after that, I was lying in the sunshine and I think I had fallen asleep, for I had a dream. I was talking with that wee baby for whom I had prayed! Often in dreams things happen that cannot take place in reality, for that little baby was talking with me, too!

"I am very happy to be here in this very safe corner of the world. It is so warm and so quiet here under Mama's heart. I have enough food and I do not at all long to be born! I am sure life must be difficult and noisy! No, I want to stay here always."

In my dream, I answered, "No, you must not think about being born as something that is sad or wrong. It is a joy to be born, for then life, the *real* life, begins. You will see your mother's face and her eyes full of love for you. You will rest in her arms; and, you will feel her arms around you. Then you will grow up and become a strong person. After you have lived for a time, there will come a moment when you have to go through another birth: when you go from this world to heaven. It will be like the time when you came from the little place under your mother's heart into life. Then you will see the eyes of Jesus and you will rest in His arms and He will bring you to a beautiful house that He has been preparing for all who believe in Him."

I awoke, and I had to laugh. But I was also

happy about that dream. It was good. I took the Living Bible and read:

> You made all the delicate, inner parts of my body, and knit them together in my mother's womb . . . . You saw me before I was born . . . .
>
> Psalms 139:13, 16 LB

Are you afraid to die? Remember that for a child of God, death is only a passing through to a wonderful new world—to the house with many mansions where Jesus has prepared a place for you.

> For we know that when this tent we live in now is taken down—when we die and leave these bodies—we will have wonderful new bodies in heaven, homes that will be ours forevermore, made for us by God himself, and not by human hands.
>
> 2 Corinthians 5:1 LB

If you don't have that assurance, please read on. I will tell you more about how to be ready.

2

The Little Lamb

It is always a tragic thing when a child dies. People have a tendency to call this an injustice on the part of God. However, God owes us nothing. If He gives our child ten years and then takes him away, we must be grateful for those ten years.

Also, I know how the Lord can use such happenings to accomplish a good purpose. I once heard about a mother who lost her child. She was very embittered and rebellious. One day she walked alone in the fields with a heavy heart. Suddenly she noticed a flock of sheep. The shepherd tried to have the sheep cross over a narrow bridge into another field, but the sheep did not want to set their feet on the shaky little bridge. They went right and left and turned just like stupid sheep do, but they did not obey the shepherd. Finally, the shepherd grabbed a little lamb that had been pressing itself against the soft wool of its mother's body. The man now carried the little lamb across the narrow bridge and put it into the meadow on the other side. Immediately, the mother sheep, bleating loudly, followed across the bridge, and then all the others followed.

The bereaved mother had observed all this with interest. Suddenly she knew that this was a message for her. She realized that for many years she had stubbornly gone her own way instead of following the call of the Good Shepherd: "Come unto me!" Now He had taken away her little son and brought him safely to the other side. His purpose was that she would come to Him, and lead the way for many others to be saved. This is what happened. She went to the Lord and gave Him her heart and life. Then she was able to be a witness to many others and help them to find the way to the Good Shepherd.

3

A Happy Visit

She was the mother of one of my club girls and had asked me to visit her in the hospital. When I arrived, she was lying in a bed in a big ward, and she was looking very happy.

"I am really having the time of my life," she said. "Never have I had such good care. I do not have to cook—they bring my meals to my bed— and the nurses even wash me. My, that is different—quite different—from being at home and taking care of my naughty boys."

I understood what she meant. She lived in a narrow alley and had a rather rough husband and many children. "Oh," she said, "it is such a joy that the nurses look after me in every way! I like being ill."

"I understand, but tell me, are you in pain?"

"Yes," she said, "I still have pain, but I must

tell you more about why I am so happy. The
woman next to me told me more about Jesus. My
daughter, who is in your club, also told me about
Him, but here I really had time to think. She gave
me a tract and a small Bible. I have been reading
them and feel so happy! She read Psalm Twenty-
three to me and I understood that the Lord *is* my
Good Shepherd. Isn't that wonderful? There is
only one almost insurmountable obstacle, and
that is that next week I must go home again. I feel
happy, but I also feel rather weak. I lost so much
blood and I do not feel strong. Then to have to go
back and start everyday life again . . . ."

I understood and said to her, "Listen. You
know now that the Lord is your Shepherd and
takes care of His sheep. When you are at home,
the same Jesus, who now gives you peace in your
heart, will be your Guide and your Friend. What
a Friend we have in Jesus! He will help you with
all the work you have to do at home. He helped
you here! When I was a little girl, five years old, I
asked Jesus to come into my heart, and He became my best Friend. Now that was a long time
ago, but I know He never lets you down. At
home, you will find that He is your teammate. Do
you have difficulties and problems?"

"Yes, I have many. Big boys are not easy these days . . . ."

I could tell her that every person in the world is very important in God's eyes and that Jesus, when He died on the cross, bore our sins and sorrows and our punishment. If she would go to Him, He would in no wise cast her out. I prayed with her, and then I heard her whisper, "Jesus, I did not know You, but I would like to be the sheep that You find and take into Your arms. Will You also forgive me my sins? Amen."

I was happy about that and again I saw that there is nobody in the world who can say, "I cannot come to Jesus, He will not accept me."

> Come unto me, all . . . .
> Matthew 11:28

He loves you and is very happy if you say, "Yes, Jesus, I want to belong to You."

> For God so loved the world, that he gave his only begotten Son, that whosoever believeth in him should not perish, but have everlasting life.
> John 3:16

4

Pain

I visited Bob, a friend who had had a terrible accident. When I entered his room, he opened his eyes and looked at me, saying only one word: "Pain." I saw on his face that his suffering was almost unbearable. I stayed with him that evening.

There came a moment when I saw that he was able to listen and I told him an experience I had in the concentration camp. "Bob, the greatest suffering I had in the concentration camp was to be stripped of all my clothing and to have to stand naked. I told my sister, 'I cannot bear this. This is worse than all other cruelties we have had to endure.' Suddenly it was as if I saw Jesus on the cross, and I remembered that it says in the Bible, 'They took His garments.' Jesus hung there naked. By my own suffering, I understood a fraction of Jesus' suffering. And that gave me strength. Now I could bear my own suffering. Love so amazing—so divine—demands my life, my soul, my all. Bob, do you realize it must have meant almost intolerable pain to Jesus to die on the cross? Just think of His hands, His feet, His body. And He did that for you and for me."

I was silent. Bob had closed his eyes. But a moment later he looked at me and said, "I am looking at Jesus. Yes, I understand only a fraction of the pain He suffered. And it makes me so thankful that He did it all for me."

Bob's face was more relaxed than before and I saw peace in his eyes. A moment later I saw that he had fallen asleep and I quietly left the room.

The next day I was able to visit him again. "Corrie," he said, "every time I had so much pain, and could hardly bear it, I was thinking of Jesus. It made me so thankful! It is as if now I have the strength to bear it. Tell me a little bit of what you thought when you had to suffer in the concentration camp. Have you ever had pain?"

"I surely have, and do you know what helped me then?

> The sufferings of this present time are not
> worthy to be compared with the glory which
> shall be revealed in us.
>
> Romans 8:18

"We can look forward to the time when we shall
be in the place where there is no pain, no cruelty,
no death. Oh, Bob, the best is yet to be! Isn't that
a joy?"

I saw him smiling for the first time. "Yes," he
said, "what a joy! The best is yet to be!"

> And God shall wipe away all tears from
> their eyes; and there shall be no more death,
> neither sorrow, nor crying, neither shall there
> be any more pain: for the former things are
> passed away.
>
> Revelation 21:4

5

Can You Forgive?

One day I visited an old friend in a hospital. When I entered her room, I saw that she was very ill, but also that there was an expression of bitterness on her face. We had many things to talk about, for we had not seen each other for a long time. Then she told me about her husband.

"I know that I will be ill for a long time. The doctor does not give me any hope that I can do my work for a long time to come. My husband did not like having a sick wife. He left me and now lives with a younger woman. He never comes to see me."

"Have you forgiven him?"

"No, I certainly have not!"

"I will tell you something of my own experiences, when I felt bitter about someone. It was in

Germany. One day I saw a lady in a meeting who
did not look into my eyes. Suddenly I recognized
her. She was a nurse who had been very cruel to
my dying sister when we were in Ravensbrück
Concentration Camp during the war. When I saw
her, a feeling of bitterness, almost hatred, came
into my heart. How my dying sister had suffered
because of her! The moment I felt that hatred in
my heart, I knew that I myself had no forgiveness. It was the Lord Jesus who said to us:

> If ye forgive not men their trespasses,
> neither will your Father forgive your tres-
> passes.
>   Matthew 6:15

"I knew I had to forgive her, but I could not.
Then I had a good talk with the Lord about it
when I was at home later. 'Lord, You know I cannot forgive her. My sister suffered too much because of her cruelties. I know, Lord, that I must
forgive, but I cannot.' Then the Lord gave me:

> The love of God is shed abroad in our
> hearts by the Holy Spirit which is given unto
> us.
>   Romans 5:5

"The Lord taught me a prayer: 'Thank You, Lord, for Romans 5:5. Thank You, Jesus, that You brought into my heart God's love by the Holy Spirit who is given to me. Thank You, Father, that Your love in me is stronger than my hatred and bitterness.' The same moment I knew I could forgive.

"I told a friend about my experience and she said, 'Oh, I know that nurse. She works in a hospital not far from here.'

" 'Can you call her?'

" 'Sure I can.' She called the nurse and I had a talk with her over the telephone, telling her that when I had the next meeting that evening, I would have a different message and would very much like her to come.

"Her answer was, 'You would like to see *me* in your meeting?'

" 'Yes, that is why I phoned. I should like it very much.'

" 'Then I will come.' She did come, and during the entire evening she looked into my eyes while I spoke. After the meeting, I had a talk with her. I told her that I had been bitter, but that God's Holy Spirit in me had brought His love instead of hatred and that now I loved her. I told her that it was through Jesus Christ who bore our sins on the cross. He forgave us, but He also fills our hearts with God's love through the Holy Spirit, and that is why I could invite her to come to the second meeting.

"I told her more and at the end of our talk that nurse accepted the Lord Jesus Christ as her personal Saviour and Lord. Do you see the miracle? I, who had hated her, was used by God to bring her to the acceptance of Jesus Christ. Not only will the Lord cleanse us by His blood but He will also use us. He used me, who hated her, and God had so absolutely forgiven and cleansed *me* that He could use me to show *her* the way of salvation!

"You are bitter about your husband, but claim Romans 5:5. I know that you love the Lord Jesus. You have known Him for a long time. Trust Him to do the miracle of bringing into your heart so much of God's love that you can forgive your husband!" I prayed with her and left.

A week later I was once more in her room. When I saw her, I knew that God had done something in her heart. "I am absolutely free. The Lord has done in me such a tremendous miracle that I could forgive my husband. You know, now there is a great peace and joy in me."

Yes, we never touch the ocean of God's love so much as when we love our enemies. It is a joy to *accept* forgiveness, but it is almost a greater joy to *give* forgiveness.

> The love of God is shed abroad in our hearts by the Holy Spirit which is given unto us.
>
> Romans 5:5

6

The Foolishness of God

After World War II, my friends and I organized a former concentration camp in Germany as a shelter for the homeless. Once, when I went there, I found a man (a lawyer) who was seriously ill. I asked him if he knew the Lord Jesus. "No," he said, "as long as I do not understand things with my brains, I cannot believe them."

I had a talk with him and I told him that in the Book of 1 Corinthians, chapters one and two tell us about the wisdom of the wise and the foolishness of God. "In the Bible," I said, "you can read very much about the foolishness of God. It is the highest wisdom. It is more important than the wisdom of the wise, because it is only through this that you get the real vision."

It was some weeks later that once more I was in our camp and I went straight to my friend. He was even more ill than the first time I had seen him. I asked, "What do you think of the foolishness of God?"

"I can praise the Lord, for I have seen that it is the greatest wisdom. I have thrown away my pride and I have come to Jesus as a sinner and asked forgiveness. I thanked Him for His death on the cross, and I can tell you that He has brought into my heart a peace that passes all understanding. It surpasses everything of the wisdom of the wise, but it is the greatest reality I have ever experienced in my life. I am so thankful for the Bible. During these weeks I have read much in it and I do not fear the future, whatever happens."

Neither death, nor life, nor angels, nor principalities, nor powers, nor things present, nor things to come, Nor height, nor depth, nor any other creature, shall be able to separate us from the love of God, which is in Christ Jesus our Lord.

Romans 8:38, 39

For the first time I saw him look really happy!

> . . . hath not God made foolish the wisdom of this world? . . . Because the foolishness of God is wiser than men; and the weakness of God is stronger than men.
>
> 1 Corinthians 1:20, 25

7

Alice

In the concentration camp, a girl once came to me and said, "Please, will you come to Alice a moment? She has such terrible nights. While we sleep, she always turns from one side to the other. She suffers. I don't know what it is. Can you help her?"

"Sure," I said, "I can help her. I can pray for her. But I am busy here with a group. We are studying a portion of the Bible. In a quarter of an hour I will come to Alice."

When I went to her, I saw that she had fallen asleep. She was very restless, tossing from one side to the other. I spoke softly to her, but she did not hear me. Then I prayed and said, "Lord Jesus, You can fill Alice's heart with Your peace. You can fill her subconscious with Your love and then she will sleep well."

As I said amen to that prayer, I saw that Alice was quiet. She slept and I knew that the Lord had answered my prayer.

The next morning, my friend who had called me the day before said, "Oh, Corrie, it was a joy that Alice slept so well. She was so quiet—and I know that God has answered your prayer."

That day Alice died, but I had enjoyed an experience that has given me much courage. When we pray, every word we say is heard by the Lord, and I even read in the Book of Revelation that our prayers are kept in heaven. Our intercession is so important!

Often we cannot reach the others, but the Lord can reach everyone. What a joy to have such a Saviour!

> . . . pray one for another . . . .
> James 5:16

8

Tommy

He was one of a big family. I believe there were fourteen children. Tommy was at a special school for mentally handicapped persons. I gave Bible lessons in that school.

Sometimes I visited Tommy in his home. When I asked where he was, his mother always said, "He's in his room upstairs." I knew where to find him—in the little corner of the attic that was his "room." It was nothing more than a bed and a chair. On the chair there was always a small picture of Jesus on the cross.

I remember that once when I visited him, Tommy was on his knees before that chair. His face was full of joy. "Tommy, why are you so happy?" I asked.

"Because Jesus loves me!" he said. "And I love

Jesus. He died on the cross for me and my sins, and now I have forgiveness."

His mother told me that Tommy always went straight to his little room when he came home. It was quiet there—a corner of peace in the rather small house. With so many children, the house was often noisy.

One day she found him with his head on the chair. In his hand was the picture of Jesus. Tommy did not move. He was with the Lord.

I'm sure that when he died, he must have felt great joy, because Jesus loved him and had died for him on the cross—and he knew it! Do you know it, too? Jesus, who loved Tommy, loves you just as much.

> For God so loved the world, that he gave his only begotten Son, that whosoever believeth in him should not perish, but have everlasting life.
>
> John 3:16

9

Toontje

In Haarlem, my hometown, there was a minister who told me of a little boy who was feeble-minded. His name was Toontje. He was always sitting in the front pew of the church. The minister said to his wife, "Toontje doesn't understand one word of my sermons. Nevertheless, he is so faithful—he comes every Sunday."

Once the pastor spoke of the ocean of God's love and told how we knew of it through Jesus Christ. When he was talking, he saw on Toontje's face an expression of great joy. Toontje understood when he talked about God's love. I myself worked among the feebleminded and know from experience that you can never speak too much about the love of God.

The next day the pastor went to Toontje's home. He thought he would see if the boy still knew something of God's love. But when he arrived at Toontje's house, he heard that the boy had died in his sleep. The pastor told me that on Toontje's dead face was an expression of heavenly joy. "I believe," he said, "that Toontje tried to get too much of God's love into his heart, so that his heart just broke for joy."

If you and I would also accept too much of God's love, our hearts could break for joy. But in heaven we shall have such strong hearts that they will contain much, much more of the love of God. Oh, what a joy that will be! Then we shall praise and thank Him for all He was and is and shall be, for us. Hallelujah! What a Saviour!

> We can only see a little of the ocean
>   when we stand at the rocky shore,
> But out there, beyond the eye's horizon,
>   there's more—there's more!
>
> We can only see a little of God's loving,
>   a few rich samples of His mighty store,
> But out there, beyond the eye's horizon,
>   there is more—there is more!
>
> AUTHOR UNKNOWN

We can read in the Bible:

When I think of the greatness of this great plan, I fall on my knees before the father from whom all fatherhood, earthly or heavenly, derives its name, and I pray that out of the glorious richness of his resources he will enable you to know the strength of the Spirit's inner reinforcement—that Christ may actually live in your hearts by your faith. And I pray that you, firmly fixed in love yourselves, may be able to grasp with all Christians how wide and deep and long and high is the love of Christ—and to know for yourselves that love so far beyond our comprehension. May you be filled through all your being with God himself! Now to him who by his power within us is able to do infinitely more than we ever dare to ask or imagine—to him be glory in the Church and in Christ Jesus forever and ever. Amen!

Ephesians 3:14–21

(*See* PHILLIPS.)

10

Mother

I would like to tell you a little bit about my mother. I loved her so very much. The last years of her life, she was very ill and she could not even talk well—only a few words. But she could love and she could receive love. It was before she fell ill that we had a talk about the Lord.

Mother said, "I am not quite sure if everything is alright between the Lord and me. My faith is so little."

I told her words of Jesus, such as, "Come unto me, all . . . ." I said, "Mother, you, too, belong to the *all*."

Mother looked sad and answered, "Yes, but . . . ." These words so often interfere when the Lord speaks to us, if we listen more to the spirit of doubt than to the Lord.

And now Mother was ill. She had had a stroke

and could only say a few words. One day, I brought her a breakfast tray. She folded her hands and then shook her head. I asked, "Mother, can you not even find words when you pray?"

"No." But then she looked at me and I saw that her face was relaxed and happy.

"But it does not matter that you cannot talk to the Lord," I said. "He talks to you, doesn't He?"

"Yes," she said, and her face was beaming with joy.

"Is it alright with you and the Lord?"

"Absolutely!" was her reply.

I tried to find out the reason she was so changed from doubt to trust. "Did we say something, Mother? Or did someone else who visited you, perhaps the pastor who came to see you yesterday? Or was it a message over the radio that gave you the assurance of salvation?"

Mother smiled and then she pointed upward with her finger.

"Was it the Lord who made it alright?"

"Yes, absolutely, it was the Lord." Six words Mother said, and what a joyful sentence!

My! There I saw that even when we could not reach her, the Lord could always reach her. And

He is more concerned about our well-being than we are for each other. When I told Father, he said, "Oh, this is an answer to my prayer!"

"Did you also pray for it? I did, too." We found out that the whole family had been praying that the Lord might give Mother great assurance instead of doubt. How He had answered that prayer! What a joy it was!

Later on, Mother grew worse and was very, very ill; then she could not talk at all. It was as if she had no consciousness, but I felt her pulse and then I talked and asked her some questions. Her heartbeat went quicker when I spoke. "Mother, when you are going to die, you have nothing to fear, for you know that Jesus died on the cross for the sins of the whole world, and also for your sins. And, Mother, He is preparing a beautiful house for you in heaven. Then you may go there and we shall see each other again. For the Lord loves us and we all love Him! Just think of it, Mother, in heaven we shall have no pain. There will be no sickness at all, and, Mother, there you will see Jesus. What a joy it will be to look at His wonderful face!"

I knew that although she could not speak at all,

she had understood what I had said. But do you understand what made me happiest? To know that when we cannot reach the other one, the Lord can reach His beloved. And it is He who has said:

> Lo, I am with you alway, even unto the end
> of the world.
>
> Matthew 28:20

I know that He was with Mother when she died and went home. He Himself brought her into His wonderful paradise. "Promoted to Glory," the Salvation Army people say.

> Thou hast beset me behind and before, and
> laid thine hand upon me.
>
> Psalms 139:5

11

Pietje

Pietje was a hunchback. She was one of my club girls. We liked each other and had a lot of fun. She could neither walk very far nor very fast and I also had difficulty keeping pace with the other girls of my club. I remember we were on a trip one time through Germany, and we had to cross a rather high mountain. Pietje came to me and said, "Auntie, give me your hand and I will help you." We both had to laugh, for she understood that I needed her help and she needed mine, so we stayed a little behind the rest of my healthy club girls and went arm-in-arm up the mountain.

Yes, Pietje was a dear girl. I remember that in the youth hostel where we stayed that evening, we had a talk about the Judgment Day of God.

Pietje said, "I'm afraid to come before the Judgment seat. Have we any advocate who will plead for us?"

"Well, just look in the Bible."

> Christ . . . maketh intercession for us.
> Romans 8:34

"That is good!" Pietje said. "Who is our judge?"

"Read it yourself."

> Who is he that condemneth? It is Christ . . . .
> Romans 8:34

"What? Jesus Christ is our Judge *and* our Advocate? Now I am not afraid anymore! He will plead us Not Guilty."

That girl was so happy because she saw what a joy it is that Jesus died for us on the cross and carried our punishment. She knew that one day He will be our Judge and our Advocate. Yes, that was a good talk we had together, there in that youth hostel! I remember there was a lovely view over the mountains and the sun was setting with beautiful colors.

Later, I had to visit Pietje when she was very ill. I found her in the corner of a huge ward in a big hospital. When I saw her, there was nobody with her—no visitors and no nurse—and I talked with her.

"Will you stay with me until I die?" she asked.

"Yes," I said, "I'll do that. Are you sure that you will die soon?"

"Yes," Pietje smiled. "I'm not at all afraid, for, you know, my Judge is the Advocate and my Advocate is the Judge. I am not afraid at all, because it is Jesus Himself who loves me and I love Him."

Say, do *you* sometimes fear when you think of the Judgment Day of God, where we all have to appear whether we believe it or not? Read your Bible! Jesus is *your* Judge and *your* Advocate. Isn't that good? We have nothing to fear— *nothing*!

Who is he that condemneth? It is Christ that died, yea rather, that is risen again, who is even at the right hand of God, who also maketh intercession for us.

Romans 8:34

12

Debbie

A friend of mine told me about her sister Debbie. She was very ill and needed some comfort. "I know," my friend said, "that you cannot go all the way to Missouri to visit her, and she cannot come to you. But what about having a talk over the telephone?" That was a good idea. Isn't it wonderful to live in a world where you can talk with each other over the telephone?

It was a good conversation. She told me her difficulties and her worries. "Corrie," she said, "I'm very ill, and some people think I must die. I am afraid of death. Can you help me?"

"Yes, surely, but listen. We haven't much time to talk over the telephone, so let us just ask each other some questions and give answers. Do you know the Lord Jesus? I don't ask if you know *about* Him, but do you *know* Him?"

"I'm not sure. I have not read much in the Bible. I did not go to church and was really not greatly interested in spiritual things, so I feel that I do not really know Jesus."

"Then first of all you must come to Him, for He is the One who can comfort and help you. He said:

> Come unto me, all ye that labour and are
> heavy laden, and I will give you rest.
>
> Matthew 11:28

> . . . him that cometh to me I will in no
> wise cast out.
>
> John 6:37

"And when you come to Him He is willing to come so close that He will even come into your heart.

> Behold, I stand at the door, and knock: if
> any man hear my voice, and open the door, I
> will come in . . . .
>
> Revelation 3:20

"Do you understand that *you* must open the door? Then He will come in and you can tell Him everything. He understands far more than I—or any other human being—can. It is true that when you come into contact with the Lord Jesus, you will see your sins, but look at the cross then. You must simply say, 'Lord Jesus, forgive me. I thank You that You died on the cross for my sins.' The Bible says that then He will cast your sins into the depths of the sea, forgiven and forgotten. And I believe that He adds a sign that reads NO FISH-ING ALLOWED! What about that?"

"I will think about it."

"No, listen! It is alright to think about it, but we have so little time now. Why not do it?"

"Do what?"

"Ask Jesus to come into your heart!"

"Is it so simple?"

"Yes, so simple!"

Then I prayed with her. Oh, it is such a joy that we can always pray with one another over the telephone—the line to the Lord is never busy. He is always ready to listen. "Lord, Debbie would like to ask You to come in, and I thank You, Lord, that You are willing. Will You send away all the doubt, all the 'yes, buts' and the 'if onlies'? I thank You, Lord, that You love Debbie. Hallelujah! Amen!

"Now, Debbie, the way is open. Say, 'Come into my heart, Lord Jesus.' "

And she did. I heard her say, "Lord Jesus, come into my heart. I know that I am not good enough, but, oh, Lord, how I need You! Thank You, Jesus, that You came into my heart. I will tell You all the sins I can remember and I thank You that You have borne them on the cross. Oh, Lord Jesus, You love me, thank You. And I love You. Amen."

Now, wasn't that a wonderful prayer? I was so happy and I know the Lord was happy. I could imagine Him standing there with His arms wide open. I said also, "Debbie, now tell Him all your fears and problems and be sure that when you feel very ill, the Lord Jesus is with you. He will not let you down for one moment."

"Are you sure?"

"Yes, for I know the Lord. I have known Him for a long time and He never gives in. And you two will win, Jesus and you. Bye, Debbie. Until we meet, not in Missouri, but there—in heaven."

"Thank you, Corrie."

I was so happy about that telephone call. But I could do something more for her, and that was to pray! And I did: "Lord, make her very conscious

of Your presence. And, Lord, surround her with
Your angels and let her room be a room where
she is together with You and the angels."

Some time afterward, I met her sister again and
she said, "Oh, Corrie, very shortly after you had
spoken with Debbie, she became more ill and I
went to her to be with her until the end. She
repeated all you had said over the telephone. 'I
did it,' Debbie told me. 'I didn't understand everything but I know that He came, for since that
time there has been such peace and joy and there
is no fear at all. I know that I have to die soon, but
do you know that I long to go to be with the Lord
in heaven?' "

What a blessed telephone talk that was!

> Jesus did it,
> The Bible tells it,
> I believe it.
> That settles it!

Come unto me, all ye that labour and are
heavy laden, and I will give you rest.

Matthew 11:28

13

Passing the Baton

You know that I am a *Tramp for the Lord*. I traveled all over the world to tell others about the Lord Jesus. I am already old and I do not like to go alone. That is why I always have a younger woman with me. At one time, the Lord gave me Connie to accompany me. For more than seven years, we went together over a large part of the world. But she married, and then the Lord gave me another companion.

There came a time when Connie became very ill, and she knew that she had to die.

Her husband came home one evening and saw that she was crying. He put his arm around her and asked, "Connie, why do you cry?"

She answered, "I traveled much with Tante Corrie and after that I traveled much with you. But now I must go on a journey all alone and you and Tante Corrie will not be with me . . . ."

"Oh, but listen Connie," said her husband. "I
will keep your hand in mine, and in the moment
when you really die, I will give your hand into
the hand of Jesus. He will keep you through the
valley of the shadow of death and bring you to the
beautiful heaven where He has prepared a house
for you!"

Connie did not cry anymore. What her husband
had said was so true! And it all happened that
way when Connie went home.

Oh, that loving hand of God! The men who
wrote the Psalms knew much when they wrote
what the Holy Spirit told them:

> If I take the wings of the morning, and
> dwell in the uttermost parts of the sea; Even
> there shall thy hand lead me, and thy right
> hand shall hold me.
>
> Psalms 139:9, 10

> . . . thou art my strength. Into thine hand
> I commit my spirit.
>
> Psalms 31:4, 5

Connie had a husband who was with her until
the last moment of her life. Many, many people

have no husband who is able and has the opportunity to stay with them when they are dying, but the great joy is that everyone can know there is a Saviour in Jesus Christ. "What a Friend we have in Jesus!" His hand keeps us, not only when we go through the valley of the shadow of death but also before that. When we pray, "Take my hand, Lord, and hold me tight," the Lord does it. He has every opportunity and every possibility—and how much love He has for us! He is never too busy with others. He takes time to be with us. He himself said:

> Lo, I am with you alway, even unto the end
> of the world.
>
> Matthew 28:20

My father used to say to us, when we were children and had to go away from home for a while, "Children, don't forget, when Jesus takes your hand, then He holds you tight. And when Jesus keeps you tight, He guides you through life. And when Jesus guides you through life, one day He brings you safely home."

14

Used by God

Once I slept in a hospital in a concentration camp. Many people were ill and many died. In the night, I heard people calling and I went to them. I was ill myself, but not so seriously that I couldn't do this—I went to everyone who called. I saw much, much suffering and loneliness there.

It was in that concentration camp hospital that I experienced God's use of sick people to help others around them. You can feel so weak in illness and unable to do anything, but witnessing for the Lord Jesus is possible because it is really the Lord who witnesses *in us* and it causes us to relax. When we are channels of living water, then it is the Lord who tells us what to say, and He *never* makes a mistake.

Nobody was with these dying people, but I

could tell all of them, "Jesus is here. Just put
your hand in His hand." And many of them
did. And then I saw peace coming into the
hearts of these people. There is a little poem in
Holland:

> *Als wij de doodsvallei betreen,*
> *laat ons elke aardse vriend alleen,*
> *maar, Hij, de beste Vriend in nood,*
> *geleid ons over graf en dood.*

When we enter into the valley of the shadow of
    death,
all our earthly friends leave us alone,
but He, the best Friend in need,
accompanies us through the grave and death.

Yes, even for people who are surrounded by
friends and relatives, a moment comes when they
have to turn to Jesus—the only One who can help
them. But what a joy that He is there!

I saw a nurse who looked so worried and tired.
Every time she passed my bed, a woman next to
me smiled to her, and sometimes she said a kind
word.

In the evening the nurse came to her and said, "Do you know that you have helped me? My day was full of disappointments, but your smile has encouraged me."

I learned an important lesson that evening.

15

Nobody Is Too Bad

During the war in Vietnam, I was permitted to visit a hospital. I talked to the men who were wounded. In a ward with about twelve patients, I had an opportunity to speak. I told them about the living Jesus, who is with us, who loved us so much that He died for us, and who now lives for us. He is at the same time at the right hand of the Father, praying for us. I also told them that He said:

> Come unto me, all ye that labour and are heavy laden, and I will give you rest.
>
> Matthew 11:28

I showed them what a joy it was that we could come to Him.

Afterwards, I had a talk with the man sitting

next to me. He was not much more than a boy,
and seriously wounded. He said to me, "What
you told about Jesus is so beautiful, so joyful! But
I cannot do what you said and go to Him. I have
heard about the Lord, but I have always blas-
phemed. When there were boys in my class who
followed the Lord, I teased them. There has been
hatred in my heart—hatred against God—and
now I know that I am seriously wounded. But I
have been too bad, I cannot go to the Lord. I am
ashamed of what I have done, of how I have tried
to keep others away from Him. Now don't tell me
that I can ask Him to help me. I am a very wicked
fellow."

"There is only one kind of person who cannot
come to Jesus," I told him. "They are the ones
who think and say, 'I'm so good, I don't need
forgiveness, I don't need the Saviour.' They are
the Pharisees, and you can read in the Bible that
Jesus could not and would not help the people
who were so proud of themselves and who
thought they were so good.

"You are quite different. You think you are too
bad. You are not. Jesus bore the sins of the whole
world and that is a lot. He has also borne your
sins on the cross: sins of hatred, of blasphemy, of

whatever you did. You *can* go to Him. Jesus hates sins but loves sinners, and all His promises are really for sinners only. *You* are not good enough; *you* are not able. It is *Jesus* who is able and He is your Saviour. Just talk to Him! Tell Him what you have done and what you have been, and then ask forgiveness. The Bible says that when you bring your sins to Him, He will blot them out like a cloud. Did you see that cloud this morning? It is gone. It will never come again. It has absolutely disappeared forever. So when you bring your sins to Jesus, He will make them disappear—He will destroy them forever and ever."

Suddenly I saw that all the men in the ward were listening. I asked, "Who of you will now come to Jesus as a sinner? When you know you are a sinner, you are forgiven." Many men in that ward responded.

If we confess our sins, he is faithful and just to forgive us our sins, and to cleanse us from all unrighteousness.

1 John 1:9

16

Niwanda

I saw a little paper in my hand. I don't know who put it there, but it was a letter: "Please, come to me. I am in the fifth bed at the right. Niwanda."

I was in Africa and had spoken that morning in a boys' boarding school. I asked the missionary if he could help me find out from whom that letter had come. He smiled and said, "Yes, I know. That boy is very ill. We could not yet take him to the hospital. Fifth bed, that is in room three. I can take you there."

We entered the room where we found Niwanda. Immediately I saw that he was really ill. "I needed some help to find you, boy!"

We both laughed and the missionary said, "I will leave you alone with him."

Niwanda and I had a good talk together. "Tell me something of yourself, boy."

"I am very ill. I have been a Christian for a long time and I have served God, but when I look back on my life, I feel so ashamed. I read in the Bible that Paul said, 'I have fought a good fight.' When I look at the past, I know that I, too, have really done my best to fight the good fight. But no, I didn't make a good job of it as Paul did."

"Listen, Niwanda. It is true that Paul wrote, 'I have fought the fight.' We can quite agree because we have such great respect for him. But he did not write, 'I have fought the fight the right way.' He means, 'I have been fighting in the good fight.' You and I also have to do so—we are both in the good fight. We stand on victory ground, because our fight is under King Jesus, and King Jesus is Victor. He makes us more than conquerors."

I saw that the boy looked happy when I told him this about fighting while standing on victory ground.

> I have fought a good fight, I have finished my course, I have kept the faith.
>
> 2 Timothy 4:7

17

His Sheep

Some time ago, I visited a friend of mine. He was a man who had often helped me. When I could not understand something in the Bible, he told me what it meant. He knew a great deal. He knew the Lord. However, there was one strange thing—he was afraid to die.

Now I had heard that he was very ill, so I went to him, thinking that I must try to help him so that he would no longer be afraid to die. It was possible that that moment would soon come. It would be such a pity if he should be afraid, since he had known the Lord for such a long time. I prayed in my heart, "Oh, Lord Jesus, will You touch him, will You take away all fear from his heart?"

When I entered his room, he looked very happy. I asked him, "Are you a little better?"

"No," he said, "I'm very weak and I know that

I must die. But what I'm so very happy about is that Jesus said, 'I give My sheep life eternal!' It is good He said it, for I cannot do anything myself. I am so tired that I cannot think properly, but I know that He will take care of me—even . . . even now. I cannot do it, but He is able."

How good it was to see that all the fear had disappeared. The Lord Himself takes care of His own. When there are moments that are difficult, we do not have to fear anything, for He is able to help us. He is faithful. He loves us.

Yes, He gives, and all that we have to do—is accept! Not one of our prayers is lost. All our prayers are kept in heaven.

Another angel came and stood at the altar, having a golden censer; and there was given unto him much incense, that he should offer it with the prayers of all saints upon the golden altar which was before the throne.

Revelation 8:3

18

Little Angel

In a children's hospital, I stood with my hand in a mother's hand. Her little girl had died. She looked like a little angel. On that little girl's dead face there was such an expression of peace!

"Oh, what joy it must be for that little child to be with Jesus! She will be so happy in heaven."

"I believe that, too," the mother said, "but Corrie, you don't know how wounded I am. I loved my little girl so very much. Why did the Lord take her away from me?"

"I do not know, but God knows. He understands you. He loves you and He loves that little girl."

There are moments when the suffering is so deep that one can hardly talk to a person. What a joy it is then to know that the Lord understands. No pit is so deep that the Lord is not deeper

still. Underneath us are the everlasting arms—
and the Lord understands.

> He shall cover thee with his feathers, and
> under his wings shalt thou trust: his truth
> shall be thy shield and buckler.
>
> Psalms 91:4

19

The Lost Sheep

Recently I met someone who had known the Lord for a long time, but she had turned away from Him. I sang to her, "What a Friend We Have in Jesus."

"I sang that song when I was in Sunday school," she said. "Yes, then I heard about the Lord Jesus every Sunday, but I have gone astray. I did not speak to Him and I did not listen to Him for many years. And now I'm so ill—what can I do?"

I told her of the good shepherd who had a hundred sheep and one of them had also gone astray. "It did not come home with the others. That shepherd left the ninety-nine at home and went to seek that one silly sheep that had lost its way. He found it, took it in his arms, and brought it home. He was very, very happy. So Jesus is on

His way looking for you. Won't you let yourself be found by this wonderful Friend who is our Saviour? He is looking for you, and when you call Him, He will take you and carry you home. He will be so happy!"

She closed her eyes and thought about it. Then, opening her eyes again, she said, "Is it as simple as all that?"

"Yes, it is."

She folded her hands. "Lord Jesus, forgive me for having gone my own way. Take me in Your arms and take me back home. Amen."

He was so near that it was as if we heard Him say, ". . . him that cometh to me I will in no wise cast out" (John 6:37).

She looked up and smiled a very happy smile. "What a Friend we have in Jesus!"

20

Worry

"Oh, my children! My husband! How can they live without me?"

I was in a hospital in a large town in the United States, and my friend Ann was very ill. She knew it and she did not tell me about her suffering, but about the greatest worry she had. "Just imagine that I should die—who would take care of my family?" I held her hand in mine and just prayed for her. Then suddenly, I remembered a little poem.

Said the Robin to the Sparrow:
"I should really like to know
Why these anxious human beings
Rush around and worry so."

Said the Sparrow to the Robin:
"Friend, I think that it must be

That they have no heavenly Father
Such as cares for you and me."
                                    ELIZABETH CHENEY

The Bible tells us:

Look at the birds in the sky. They neither
sow nor reap nor store away in barns and yet
your heavenly Father feeds them.
                                    See Luke 12:24

Aren't you much more valuable to Him than they
are? Can any one of you, however much he worries, make himself an inch taller? And why do
you worry about clothes? Consider how the flowers grow. They neither work nor weave, but I tell
you that even Solomon in all his glory was never
arrayed like one of these. Now, if God so clothes
the flowers of the field which are alive today and
discarded tomorrow, is He not much more
likely to clothe you—you of little faith? Don't
worry at all, then, about tomorrow. Tomorrow
can take care of itself. One day's trouble is
enough for one day.

I could easily understand that her children and
her husband were reasons to worry about the fu-

ture. However, our times are in God's hands, and He loves her family even more than she loved them. Worrying is carrying tomorrow's load with today's strength—carrying two days at once. It is moving into tomorrow ahead of time. Worrying does not empty tomorrow of its sorrow—it empties today of its strength.

"Do you know, Ann, I do not believe that worry is from the Lord. It is from the enemy. There has been a man upon the earth of whom Satan is afraid, a man whom he can neither touch nor resist—Jesus Christ. And that is why we can go to Him for help. You are not able to overcome worry, but the Lord Jesus can, and He will—through His Holy Spirit. When we see that worry is a sin—and that is what it really is, for the Bible tells us not to worry—then we know what to do with sin, don't we?"

"Yes, we take it to the Lord, and when we confess our sins, the blood of Jesus cleanses us from all of our sins."

"That is true, so just ask forgiveness for having worried, and then ask Jesus to keep worry away. He gives us peace under all circumstances. I have a little stick here that cannot stand on my hand by itself. But I can even let it stand on the top of my finger, if my hand holds it. In the same way, we cannot keep worry away, but when we surrender to the wounded hands of Jesus, He keeps us from falling. One day He will present us blameless and with unspeakable joy. That will be on the day when He will reveal Himself. Jesus is stronger than all of our problems."

I prayed with Ann and then she said, "I have much to think about and I know one thing—I am not able, but Jesus is. He will do the job."

Cast thy burden upon the Lord, and he shall sustain thee: he shall never suffer the righteous to be moved.

Psalms 55:22

21

Our Times Are in God's Hands

It is a feast for me to be in Holland, for I meet friends of former days. I gather them in my home to tell them how much I have experienced during the last year. At one of these gatherings, I missed one of my friends. Somebody told me, "She is ill, so she could not come."

I went to see her. She told me what had happened. "I have been very ill, and everyone—myself, too—thought I had to die. Oh, Corrie, I was not afraid. I was just thinking about the joy of seeing the Lord Jesus as I read in the Bible all the promises that speak of heaven. But then I began to recover. I am not strong, but the doctor said that in a short while I shall be able to do my work again."

"Are you happy?"

"Yes. I can be an eternity in heaven and there is much work for me to do here in this world. I believe I will return to my everyday life richer than I was before I was ill. I see now that our times are in God's hands. I believe I will take the good opportunities, which the Lord will give me in the future, with more thankfulness, because I had thought I had lost them forever. I knew, when I was dying, how serious my condition was, but the Lord gave me grace. I was not afraid. Now I know, as I go back to my everyday life, that I will see the smaller problems in the light of eternity. I am sure I will not be so concerned about the problems of everyday life. I thank God that I had this illness. It made me more ready for life."

> All things work together for good to them that love God . . . .
>
> Romans 8:28

The Lord never makes a mistake. One day, when we are in heaven, I'm sure we shall see the answers to the *whys*. My, how often I have asked, *"Why?"* In heaven we shall see God's side of the embroidery. God has no problems—only plans. There is never panic in heaven.

22

When I Saw Death

When I heard that my father had died in prison, I was alone in a cell. The prisoner who had been in the cell before me had written on the wall NOT LOST, BUT GONE BEFORE.

After the first shock, I realized what a great joy it was for Father to be with the Lord in the beautiful place that Jesus had prepared for him. Straight from the cell in a prison to that place of peace and love of God. I could thank the Lord that He had taken him home. Yes, he was not lost but gone before.

When I saw Betsie after she had died in the ward of the concentration camp, I saw an expression of intense joy and peace on her face. She even looked young. I could only thank and praise the Lord that He had taken her to Himself. It was as if her face reflected a little bit of the tremendous joy that her soul experienced at that moment, when she went to be with the Lord.

I looked death in the eyes several times myself, and when fear came into my heart I told the Lord Jesus. He did not give me a spirit of fear, but of power and of love and of a sound mind. I knew that I did not have to pass through the valley of the shadow of death alone. Jesus was with me.

The moment I was almost sure that death was coming was when my number was called out when we were standing on roll call. I had to stand as number one in the front row. Many of us thought—also I myself—that we had been called out because they were going to kill us.

I stood there for three hours, and next to me was a Dutch girl I had never seen before. I said to myself: "This is now the last person on earth to whom I can bring the Gospel." And I did. She told me her life story. I told her that Jesus loved her and that He had given His life on the cross to bear her punishment. That girl said *yes* to Jesus.

I was not killed, I was set free.

What do you think about death, about the death of your loved ones, and of yourself? Study the Bible, the answer is there. Talk with the Lord, He understands and loves you. When you come to Him, He will in no wise cast you out or send you away. Are you afraid? Give your fear to Him.

23

Are You Afraid to Die?

In Chicago I met an old friend of mine. I had not seen him for a long time, and I was spending only one day in his town. We had a good talk together, and I remember that I asked him a question. "Are you afraid to die?"

"Yes, I am," he said.

His answer surprised me. He loved the Lord and had known Him a long time. He had a deep faith in God. "Why are you afraid to die? You have been a Christian as long as I have known you. Surely you know that Jesus will not leave you alone for one moment."

"I am afraid, Corrie, because I have never died before. I am afraid because I do not know what it is like to die."

Then we talked about Jesus. Before He went to

the Cross, He had never died either. Was He also a little afraid?

But today Jesus knows what it is like to die. He has already been through death, and today Jesus says to you and to me, "I will never leave you nor forsake you," and "Lo, I am with you always." That means *even* death.

The old man smiled and said, "Isn't God good to us—that we could talk and think together about this today?"

"Are you afraid to die?"

Fear thou not; for I am with thee: be not dismayed; for I am thy God: I will strengthen thee; . . . yea, I will uphold thee with the right hand of my righteousness.

Isaiah 41:10

No temptation has overtaken you that is not common to man. God is faithful, and he will not let you be tempted beyond your strength, but with the temptation will also provide the way of escape, that you may be able to endure it.

1 Corinthians 10:13 RSV

"Are You Going Home?"

Are you going Home to be with the Lord?
You are not afraid, are you?

Afraid of what?
To feel the Spirit's glad release,
to pass from pain to perfect peace,
the strife and strain of life to cease?
Afraid of that?

Afraid of what?
Afraid to see the Saviour's face?
To hear His welcome and to trace
the glory gleam from wounds of grace?
Afraid of that?

Afraid of what?
To enter into heaven's rest
and yet, to serve the Master blessed,
from service good to service best?
Afraid of that?

Think of stepping on shore and finding it heaven, or taking hold of a hand and finding it God's, or breathing new air and finding it celestial, or feeling invigorated and finding it immortality; of passing through a tempest to a new and unknown ground; of waking up well and happy and finding it home.

You Have His Word

My sheep hear my voice, and I know them, and they follow me: And I give unto them eternal life; and they shall never perish, neither shall any man pluck them out of my hand.

John 10:27, 28

I am the resurrection and the life: He who believes in me will live, even though he dies.

John 11:25 NIV

The gift of God is eternal life through Jesus Christ our Lord.

Romans 6:23

Blessed be the God and Father of our Lord Jesus Christ, which according to his abundant mercy hath begotten us again unto a lively hope by the resurrection of Jesus Christ from the dead, To an inheritance incorruptible, and undefiled, and that fadeth not away, reserved in heaven for you.

1 Peter 1:3, 4

What we suffer now is nothing compared to
the glory he will give us later.

Romans 8:18 LB

No mere man has ever seen, heard or even
imagined what wonderful things God has ready
for those who love the Lord.

1 Corinthians 2:9 LB

If we confess our sins, he is faithful and just
to forgive us our sins, and to cleanse us from
all unrighteousness.

1 John 1:9

Forasmuch as ye know that ye were not re-
deemed with corruptible things, as silver and
gold, from your vain conversation received by
tradition from your fathers; But with the pre-
cious blood of Christ, as of a lamb without
blemish and without spot.

1 Peter 1:18, 19

But God commendeth his love toward us, in
that, while we were yet sinners, Christ died for
us.

Romans 5:8

Verily, verily, I say unto you, He that heareth my word, and believeth on him that sent me, hath everlasting life, and shall not come into condemnation; but is passed from death unto life.

John 5:24

These things have I written unto you that believe on the name of the Son of God; that ye may know that ye have eternal life, and that ye may believe on the name of the Son of God.

1 John 5:13

For our light affliction, which is but for a moment, worketh for us a far more exceeding and eternal weight of glory.

2 Corinthians 4:17

For we know that if our earthly house of this tabernacle were dissolved, we have a building of God, a house not made with hands, eternal in the heavens.

2 Corinthians 5:1

But thanks be to God, which giveth us the victory through our Lord Jesus Christ.

1 Corinthians 15:57